It's Time

Poems

by

David Middlewood

Grosvenor House
Publishing Limited

The right of David Middlewood to be identified as the author of this
work has been asserted in accordance with Section 78
of the Copyright, Designs and Patents Act 1988

The book cover is copyright to David Middlewood
The front cover image is credited to:
www.istockphoto.com/gb/portfolio/ml1413

This book is published by
Grosvenor House Publishing Ltd
Link House
140 The Broadway, Tolworth, Surrey, KT6 7HT.
www.grosvenorhousepublishing.co.uk

A CIP record for this book
is available from the British Library

ISBN 978-1-83975-097-7

CONTENTS

PEOPLE AND PLACES

CHILDREN AND FAMILIIES

VULNERABILITY AND CARE

REFLECTIONS

PREFACE

These poems cover a period of about thirty five years, with the two main periods being from the mid 1980s to late 1990s and about 2014 to 2020. I am fully aware that they are of uneven quality, but some are included for reasons personal to myself or the person(s) concerned. Altogether, they record what has moved me, made me smile, laugh, cry or cause me to reflect, as well as some of my personal interests of course. My thanks to all the people who have inspired me, whether they were aware of it or not, those in the poems such as friends and family, and, like any other writer, I owe debts to other poets that I have admired, such as Hardy, Frost and the first one who impacted on me, Wordsworth. Some special thanks to three organisations, Symphony House, The Hope Centre and the local branch of Samaritans, all of whom have given me so many insights and perspectives. Finally, my thanks to some dear friends, Melissa, Kathy and Trish, for their assistance in the production of this work and, most of all, to my muse! Thank you with love, Jacqui !

David Middlewood   2020

LOVE AND LOSS

THE END OF ROSES

I had thought it would be the end of roses,
the end of damson blossoms in their shocking white,
in its first burst against the still nearly bare boughs.
I had thought it would be the end of budding,
the profusion of clematis over the ageing, bending arch.
I had thought it would be the end of all new life,
when I thought that you might die.

I had thought it would be the end of all soft skin,
of every line and tremor to be traced
through rougher hands on shoulders, napes or ears.
I had thought it would be the end of things unseen,
lying behind the eyes that fill so easily with wetness.
I had thought it would be the end of all todays,
when I thought that you might die.

Now that I know we have more time,
perhaps I'll see some buds push outwards into life,
covering all dark thoughts with colour and with light;
perhaps we both will see a rose unfold
and beckon us to view its blatant beauty,
and share its understanding of what's left of life.

THE RESPONSIBILITY OF LOVE

Sometimes she looks at me in such a way
on me the loving weight of her whole world it lies,
and there is nothing I can do or say;
I dare not look her in the eyes.
The pain of knowing how her life would be,
if 'life' you'd call it, with half cut away,
is in us both knowing, should she be without me,
the spirit would leave her body; where mine was, she'd stay.
Romance and love we've known, and also violent passion.
None of these is separate now; the whole thing blurs
into the being together that's shaped us in this fashion,
so that she is more than half my world, as I am hers.
So when that look comes, making my heart nearly burst,
I say to myself, 'Please let me not die first.'

CRUMPLED

He had not known that love could lie in crumpled faces,
that reaching out to touch a crumpled skin
was as erotic as the secret creases of the body,
and as tender as the dimpled furrows of a baby;
that just to look upon a crumpled face
could stir him into looking into life itself.

All his life before seemed an irrelevance,
for now he knew that it had led him to this point
where his lips and fingers on this crumpled face,
rising from crumpled sheets, took on a kind of vibrancy
and made him aware of everything within his space,
that he saw only what he was meant to see.

How could he know that love would stay in crumpled faces?
He knew because the face had taught him where to look-
in shabby railway waiting rooms, in dubious cafes,
In crumpled chairs, holding a crumpled book;
he knew he would take the crumpled face he loved
with his own crumpled body to the grave.

WINDOWS-LOOKING IN

When I was sixteen, I fell in love-with Marilyn Monroe!
Those lips, those curves, that sexy smile-my Marilyn Monroe.
She adorned my sixteen year old's books, showing off her pouty looks;
I dreamed that she and I would meet, I'd sweep her off her sexy feet,
and we'd disappear, we'd go- just me and Marilyn Monroe!

So she stayed the same on my history folder,
though I did, she could not, grow older.
Years later, when I read she'd died, I don't even think I sighed.
Later, finding the truth about her life,
her vulnerability, her insecurity and strife,
I knew I should have looked behind those eyes
and seen that all the rest of it was lies.

Then when at last I fell in love for sure,
with a gentle force that shook me to the core-
they were there, the curves, the smile, the lips and oh so special eyes,
only now straightway, I could realise
that vulnerability, that incomparable sadness of a soul
who needed loving care so much that I
was smitten, because behind the windows of the eyes
was this woman, whose soul was in the skies.

And if I ever take our life complacently,
I look through those windows, where I can see
something so fragile and it says to me,
'I am here with you, and must always be'.

ON LOOKING AT HER PHOTOGRAPH

Clever little wisp of hair
hanging down below her ear, just touching her shoulder,
you need not curl so complacently,
my hands have been there too, you know.

Smug little pearlet ear ring,
pressing firmly against her lobe,
you need not nestle so neatly;
my teeth have been there too, you know.

Saucy little nose's cyst,
hiding in its shadow, hugging her eye line,
you need not settle so smoothly;
my lips have been there too, you know.

Let me tell you, bits and pieces,
that I shall laugh last when I have her next.
You need not fear exclusion though,
for I will take you all in with me in lustful love,
and most of all a tenderness that overwhelms me
for all the rest of her no photograph can show.

ON A WIFE'S SEVENTIETH BIRTHDAY

No, it's true; age cannot wither her,
nor, though it tries, can it weather her
flawless skin. In my heart and eyes she stays
as lovely as when years ago, in earlier days,
she looked up to my face and from above
I saw those eyes telling of their sadness and a need for love.

The passing years, for all they work and strive,
they cannot remove the way we keep alive
each moment of each day which makes us move to each other,
each moment different, but oddly the same as any other.
Tomorrow, we shall love once more throughout these special hours,
but underpinned by love's renewed unending powers.

Her birthday is for us merely a chance to pause
and reflect on just how much time's laws
are meaningless to her, my Autumn Queen.
My Libran lass unparalleled has seen
so many days, so many gifts she's carried,
and most of all the gift to him she loved and married.

OUR CHILD

Although we two, who are come close on ninety five,
although we have no child, nor will while we're alive,
because of fate and late finding of each other,
clearly with me you cannot be a mother,
still we have brought a precious life into the world .
My birth, at forty three years old,
began a tale, one you helped to be told.
It brought the new you from behind those deep eyes
so that our late summer we could realise.

Now love IS this life, and we'll live out our late season,
like any family, we'll love beyond the bounds of reason,
plucking the berries from the mottled trees and hedges,
keeping the low dark clouds away as towards us winter edges.

Our child is in those hedges and those country lanes,
in pubs with umbrellas and churches with vanes,
in sandwiches in lay-bys and damp Kent Easter beaches,
we'll cherish it as ourselves, until at last it reaches
our time for sleeping, away from this world's wild,
and settle down at peace, just you, me and our child.

DRIVING BACK HOME IN AUTUMN

There was nothing unusual about the drive,
on a Friday evening in early November,
driving along the dual carriageway,
my thoughts on the weekend and easy chairs.

I became aware of the most unheavenly sky;
not just a patch of Autumn's vibrant redness,
but a kaleidoscope of purple and grey
and crimson drifting into indescribable forms.

That sky was meant to be seen from mountains,
by shepherds, tribesmen, wanderers and seers,
yet somehow I , in my metallic box, was one of those
chosen to see, if only I would use my inner eye.

I could believe for a half mile of my journey
that the roadside lights were stars for just that sky.
Comforted by the thought of your unreal reality at home,
I drove into that world through a gap in the clouds.

COMPLETING THE PICTURE

'Always put a human figure in the scene,
to give extra interest to what else might be flat,
and lacking that something that draws us inside.'
So I snap you in the bluebell woods where we have often been
-----------and you make it complete.

The beeches' greys, as much as all the blues,
contribute to the picture, impossible to paint;
Just when I think I've captured it and every subtlety,
shimmering sunlight suddenly gives out different hues
 ---------only you make it complete.

But I know that, if you were to be away,
the scene would be just separate parts,
each beautiful , but lacking in that special tint.
This world needs you, as do I, so you must stay-
    You make it all complete.

And when I take the picture home with me,
I can take the blues, the greens, the hues, the trees,
the shimmering sunlight and the fallen branches,
and keep it in the album of my heart for both of us to see.
    You make it all complete.

A MOMENT IN HISTORY

Overflowing with colour, scent, herbs, fruit and green,
this garden with its high Victorian wall
provides the setting for this historic scene;
the yellows, purples, pinks and reds, they all
seem to stimulate the noisy birds to call
to each other or perhaps to us.

Flash forward fifty years-the wall will hold,
as it has done for a hundred and sixty years to date;
fashion or environmental need will have told
its story on this form of scene and its fate
is settled; any wishes we had now too late,
for others and for us.

Perhaps all buildings then will have their plaque
recording what adventures have been here told.
Only through two centuries by then looking back,
will there be awareness of how old
has been the story that they then unfold
including ours?

But what it won't record-etched on or written by the wall
is the most momentous moment of them all,
that we two sat in silent love and were as one,
as together we drank in the colours and the sun.

WRITE ME A POEM

'Write me a poem', my love said to me;
she meant like the ones of earlier years.
Has too much contentment sated my muse?
Or is it something else she fears?

Might she be right? Together we have found
shared meanings in both the petty and the fine.
We both know her baking here today-fresh scones-
is saying , 'Love is in a poem- here is mine.'

So how do I tell her that her look
and her smile, her nose, her eyes, her ear,
every familiar trace of her face
still move me as ever and blots out any fear,
the fear of a lover that one far-off day,
either the one of us will not be here.
Till then, this love claims both a scone and kiss,
and in return, I offer –this!

TINY THINGS

Each morning from the bed she rises,
while I still drowsily stir in my side's place,
walks round the bed towards the mirror,
pats both cheeks and says, with me half hearing,
'Come on, wake up, face!'

Why this is so alluring
I cannot explain.

They make no sense to anyone-including me-
the tiny things that make the life we feel and see;
you only know the pain if they go missing-
they seem so much more than any kissing.

THE SEAT AT THE END OF THE PATH

'What is that path?'
'It is our path.'
'What is that seat?'
'It is our seat.'
'Why is it there?'
'It is there for us.
We shall sit together
and see the colours,
the flowers and the view.
We shall see where we have come from,
and the journeys we have still to make.'
'When will the path end?'
'When we end.'
'When will we end?'
'When the path ends.
Do you not see?
The seat is for two.'

WALK WITH ME

I wish that you could walk with me
along those Kentish lanes in this late Spring;
then I could show and share with you
those mass profusions of the woodlands' floors,
covered in primroses where the yellow stretches far
as your eye can see until it's lost in shade.
You'd see the slightly less obtrusive violets too,
still profuse, but more responsive when you bend to them.
I'd show you how to find the single chestnut tree,
hiding among so many less seductive rambling, bramble-hidden trees,
perhaps even a walnut or two left on the ground, no use,
but such a source of my delight because -it's there!

Later, I'd show and we'd share the harvesting of windfall fruit,
lying in uncut grass in open orchards,
selecting the gnarled and knobbly apples-best in our view—
cherries, plums, and pears, we'd eat together in their unwashed state.
In Winter, we'd struggle through the snowdrifts, five feet high,
In the lanes impassable to all but we intrepid souls.
Coming home, we'd dry sodden socks and gloves before the flames
and sit there watching how the rising stream
dissolves In nothingness, just like this dream.

CONVERGENCE

Conceived in a phoney war, they said she felt too much.
As soon as her hair could be brightly ribboned,
matching bright eyes that made the shadows light,
her feet were placed upon a path;
'Dance !' they said, 'for you are sweet and good-
but beware the shadows.'
Perhaps her eyes and ears were with the stars,
and she could not hear.
So she danced her way through school and college,
through marriage, births and stage and school again,
for more than forty years to keep shadows at bay.

Meanwhile, his more dogged pace had taken him
through woods and fields, along high-hedged lanes,
looking less often but aware of those same stars.
He had seen the shadows and he knew
they were mere reflections of things real and mostly safe.
He too had surged through marriages and births and confident career,
ever more unafraid but looking for some light.

Then, fate sent her dancing path across his more steady route;
she came into his leafy lanes, his cornfields and his trees.
They shared their bodies and their books, their love of past and poems.
She found at last there was a shade to shelter in,
resting against its source of actual blood and flesh,
while he, encircling her, finally found that light in their convergence.

THE EMPTY MIRROR

I look into the mirror from my side of the bed,
where, each morning, I saw both her back and face;
but then it dawned on me she's no longer there,
when its blankness gives me nothing back but space.
Wait-there's a face there-was it all a bad dream?
No , it's my ghastly presence, all bleak-eyed and grim.
Less than half a person now blinks at the glass;
I must stare that man out-because she loved him.
I hate him and part of me wants to hate her,
for dying and leaving him in bed to grow old.
How could she do it? She should have stayed-
he knows if he touches the mirror, it's cold.
But if I turn over , face away, even worse,
Her side of the bed is as cold as my curse.

THERE BUT NOT THERE

I stood at the window today,
watching the slanting rain and the grey skies-
and I saw your two eyes.
Strangely, they looked just like the circles
made by the rain in the puddles outside.
I think you know what I mean.

I stood under a tree in the park today,
the sleet biting my face and my hand,
when I saw you by the stand.
Strangely, you looked just like a dog,
its hair soaked, barefoot in the grass.
I think you know what I mean.

I walked from the park to go back home again,
and saw you were the black slates glistening in the wet,
and saw you were the mud tyre tracks, fresh and never set.
You were the spiked black railings of that old school;
you looked like two bright mops outside a door,
fighting against the grey.
I saw you splashing over my shoes again
and dropping off a gutter into a drain.
I think you know what I mean.

Only –when I reached the house, I looked for you –
and now I could not see you –you were not there.

A FEER

I pottered in the garden, cutting here and there;
more light in on a hidden shrub I planned to let,
when the weirdest thought swept over me-
what if we'd never met!

The flatness and the emptiness of such a life for me
so overwhelmed me, as in half- light I stood,
that I was forced to go back in the house
to know you're flesh and blood.

FOR JOHN GWATKIN

(For a motor-cycling friend who died of cancer)
John, you deserved a better end,
like a motor cycle crash on a TT bend,
a skid , tyres' squeal, a short sharp cry,
as you joined those bikers in the sky.

Of course it would have pained us all
not to be there at your final fall;
we'd have had no chance to say goodbye
as you joined those bikers in the sky.

But better than those last drawn-out days,
when the John we knew was beyond our gaze,
when each breath was pain, as the end was nigh
for him to join those bikers in the sky.

Let the time pass, Margaret, family, friends, all;
eventually, love will help us to recall
the former John, honest , bluff and true,
less a man for words, more a man to do.
But I think of him and the gap he leaves;
among so many, I'm just one who grieves.
When we all can lift our cast-down eyes up high,
we'll see John-our biker in the sky!

WHAT PREPARATION

He died so suddenly one day, all of us quite unwarned.
'The heart', they said to his wife, guilty she'd not been there.
She, now widow, struggling for sense of what her half-life meant,
his sons disbelieving that his permanence was not.

And yet- they found his letters, written for that very day,
one for each son, separate but same. So helpful this little pack
of documents and instructions, where to find and what to do,
and so useless in that nothing in them could ever bring him back.

So, did he know that death was somehow stalking him
that he took such tender care of those he'd loved and left?
How long did he foresee, and did he agonise as how to use
what unknown length of time he had before they were bereft?
I never saw it in his eyes or heard it in his voice;
he seemed the man I'd always known, and held in huge esteem,
and now I'll never know if something lay beneath his daily mien,
or whether he lived his final years as if in a kind of dream.

THE WIDOW

Kicking up the dead leaves of memories,
as I walked yesterday,
I stumbled across your body.
Picking it up, I felt it warm in my hands
as they closed in bed over your great warm back,
your shifting bulk in the dark,
the huge protective wall against which I huddled
in brief but total shelter,
leaving me to dream of those Autumn walks together.

Now, feeling the stick cool and dampen to my touch
and to avoid awareness of its shrivelled bark,
I placed it carefully with those covering leaves
and walked quietly on,
trying not to think of the empty bed.

THE WIDOWER

I walked with you from the same car park,
through the same green,
with the same stream, through the same side-street to the city centre.

I talked with you-though you did not answer-
in the same voice,
in the same shops,
as we shared our usual moments of the day.
You did not take my arm in the usual way,
and, as we returned by the same ducks and moor hens,
I saw they were less brightly coloured than before.

Reaching our house, I could no more ignore
that, though your voice is in my ear,
and your movements flit in and out
of the shadows of my mind,
your soft but firm-lined body is no longer here-
and I am left to love your space.

NO WORDS

You're sitting so quietly in the chair facing mine;
I don't need to look at you-your presence feels there;
your eyes will be closed, their dreams are elsewhere.
Then I'm aware of your shifting, eyes blink before shine.
You stretch and you sigh, chide yourself for dozing,
'There's still things to do', you say as you slowly rise.
'You shouldn't have let me sleep - meant to close my eyes.
Your head's stuck in that book of course. Now , just supposing
I'd slept on and on, nothing ever getting done;
But then you know all about me, after all these years,
in fact, we know each other, souls , hopes and fears.'
This chatter forms a familiar backcloth to our life of two as one.
Finally, I force my face up from the page and face-the wall!
It was about a year ago that she failed to wake at all.

ON A NEPHEW DYING YOUNG

Marcus – your Roman name becomes you well,
for death without dishonour was their creed to tell.
Better, they said, to leave this world and all its woes
than stay, enduring ever more throes,
of the pain and suffering you've had to bear-
in your last days with us, more than your share.

Well, no one deserves such rest with honour more.
For nobody showed a greater courage for,
despite the pain borne over these last years,
when we view all your life-more smiles than tears.

Perhaps- we're sure- you're in a better place;
one where you can wear your special cheeky face,
where you can play those same cds incessantly-
and get one of your special pizzas set for tea!

Whilst here, your mother, father, sister, niece-
they go on loving you in your new found peace.
And all the rest of us, your family and friends,
we know you now have rest that never ends.
Think of us, Marcus, as we think of you-
till we meet again-it's just adieu!

STILL SAM

(for a grandson killed aged six years)
Always moving, such a fidget, never still,
gulping his food or slipping it to sister,
always into something new, something different to fill
the time his restless, cheeky, cheery self could seize.

Now he is still. And yet-he is still
Sam-forever restless, smiling, with that grin
caught for all time in a place that will
mean he never slows or ages like the rest of us.

He'll wait somewhere upon a distant shore,
his face forever in that perpetual grin
to say to those that love him when they come
to join him after years, 'Well, where've you bin?!'

LAMENT

They carried my husband shoulder high
when he won a TT race;
I shed tears of joy in my pride that day,
as much as if he'd walked in space.

They're carrying him shoulder high again,
six of his team are here;
the noise of the crash still fills my head,
and my eyes are too dry for a tear.

They carry him shoulder high in a box,
as on the crash day, there's rain.
They'll lower him into the ground very soon,
and we'll never hold each other again.

ON A PARENT LOSING AN
ADULT CHILD

She is gone and it is just so wrong
that she should go and leave this world before me.
In all my dreams, I never could foresee
her life so short and mine perhaps so long.
Imaginings were of my older years,
with children fondly looking to my needs,
she among them, with small routine deeds,
until I slipped away among their tears.
Because of others loved, I face the fates;
their love for me, like ours for her, will last.
We must all hold the future in what's past
as daily we move a step to where she waits.
But never could I think that this reversal
would be her death to act as my rehearsal.

ON THE LAST CHILD LEAVING HOME

You don't notice a space till it's no longer filled
with the things your eyes took for granted.
And the noise! It was always there-sometimes it spilled
from one room across to another.
Even when no one was talking, somehow you could tell
that a presence still filled the place.
When their friends were here, the rooms seemed to swell
to take all the extra ones in .
at night, when the whole of the family slept,
there seemed so much life in that quietness.
And after the first one left, that room still kept
his space and the rest closed in round it.

But now, the space! I never knew this house was so large;
each room I enter is bigger than I knew.
I go cautiously in, as if careful not to barge
in on anyone there,
only to realise I might as easily have smashed
the door down for all the difference it made.
I check upstairs and find I feel somewhat abashed
to see there's a bed not unmade or disturbed.
So this is freedom? Freedom to enjoy the emptiness of space?
I'll keep their two rooms ready always-just in case!

PEOPLE AND PLACES

THE CLOCKMENDER
(OR 'TIME STANDS STILL')

All time stands still as he carefully works away
in the small room where he methodically applies
his surgeon's skill to these various guardians of times.
The tiniest part must take its turn upon the table
waiting to be inserted and adjusted till it finds its place
back where it belongs, awaiting reassuring chimes.

Surrounded by others, patiently waiting their turn
to be re-jointed and then re-assembled,
the clocks submit to his painstaking fingers' call.
These ones have all eternity to wait in line
knowing that when at last they do rejoin the world,
they are just of that moment , with no time lost at all.

And then at last the work's complete and tried,
and this one takes its place, heading homeward queue,
and without irony, he checks upon those hours that went.
He knows his time had stopped while he was working here,
oblivious to what the world outside has counted down.
His world, and ours, is richer for that time spent.

THE SALON

A world of colour, chatter and an overpowering smell of sweet
fruits of lemon, orange and vanilla is what they meet
with 'Lovely to see you!' and 'Had a good week?'
and other such practised idioms of salonspeak.

Downstairs the toes and fingernails hasten to be painted,
ensuring that such vital organs stay untainted;
so that when the weekend's social whirl commences,
the ones they seek to pleasure lose all their senses.

The women's heads emerge from curlers, nets or domes,
like butterflies from chrysalids seeking their new homes,
or Cinderellas in their new garb casting off their rags,
while their last hours been lost in tea and glossy mags.

These women emerge renewed, seem genuinely pleased,
the pressures of the week just gone temporarily eased.
Those women who ply their craft in working there
know that it is about much more than hair-
they've swept up the stresses of their clients' last week
without which these, if unreleased, could peak
in something that might be infinitely worse;
each salon worker is both therapist and nurse.

A solitary man rises, leaving an empty coffee cup,
smiles upon his newly coiffured wife as she gets up.
He has said one word for every thousand uttered
and for an hour his mind has been completely shuttered.
But his smile is as real as any hair that's curled,
he'll be back next week -he's now part of this world!

PAST THE DAY

A graduation, a wedding, another family event,
We look fifty times at the invites thus sent.
We are too well aware that shadows will be cast
by the presence of a kind of ghost from the past.
We practise the smiles, the 'I hope you're okay'
and the rituals that help us get through the day.
We'll say all the right things, like 'It's their day, not ours,'
but the sunshine is threatened by more than just showers.
I'll say it's just a day, and that it doesn't last,
but I know in your heart that you carry that past.

Coming home from the day, we pick over its bones,
the smiles and the photos, the cheers and the moans;
you say in despair, 'I shall never be free
from my old self, the one that used to be me.'
And when we get back to what will be our tomorrow,
we try to make sense of this transient sorrow.
The truth is we live in the present; each year
is soon the past, and the future's soon here.
The sun will rise next week, just as back then it rose,
that past helped to shape us into each one we chose.
But the present and future are ours and we're free
to shape our past our way-for you and for me.

IN A CRETAN VILLAGE

High in the Cretan hills, enclosed by a wire fence,
where a few grapes are rotting on their ancient vines,
and some solitary apples mock their almost leafless trees,
and where, generations ago, local farmers plied their trade,
by the flat-roofed white- washed, weekends- only house,
and remnants of residence lie around-children's bikes,
geranium pots and wooden swings in trees,
one man toils alone with pick and spade.

The ground gives nothing that is not torn out-
piece by piece of rocky, dry, unyielding earth.
Black hair plastered to his front and back,
he fills the barrow and moves the day's reward.
About a metre's width, perhaps-to tip it in another place.
For what purpose does he punish his own body so?
Is it because it's there and therefore must be dug?
Or is it because the body needs the earth while still his back's broad?

From inside the house, the television's sound blares out,
telling of a different world. But what primeval instinct
drives him on, to give his precious hours for such small steps,
straining his body to shape this stubborn and unyielding earth?
Is it something inside him says he has no choice,
or does he have an unshared vision in his sweating head
of what was past to come again and gain back man's control,
or is this observer witnessing some new kind of birth?

GRADUATION

How many good things in life are just so short,
the ones so often that we think ought
to last longer so we can squeeze more joy
out of the moment, like a child with a toy.
Sixty seconds, perhaps less, is what we all come to see
with many travelling from afar so they can be
here for a culmination of a life's three year,
each person's single minute to them and theirs so dear.

And then 'your' moment comes, your own 'drum roll',
trying to look casual as you take your scroll;
we shout your name, we clap and cheer,
although we know you surely cannot hear.

There will be tears and smiles for you later to recall,
as you join with friends, now graduates all.
But later, when all's quiet in your own space,
you'll feel the pride but know that in its place
will come thoughts of the future, what lies ahead,
the life to be lived, more than the books you've read.
All those that love you, we all feel the same,
more than the letters now after your name,
you're still most of all the special person you are-
Veatriki Sarri, you are forever a star!

AN EVENING OF DANCE

As the evening begins and things get under way,
each family is seeking its own Margot Fonteyn;
no matter the age, they will find, come what may,
some movement to cheer for, no one will complain.
They come fast and furious, one dance then another,
each person knows how to respond to each beat,
all the time they're urged on by a father and mother.
Long hair is thrown forward in meeting bare feet.
But when you look out through your half-closed eyes,
the individuality it dies.
With focused look, more than a glance,
you lose the dancers in the dance.

The dancers all thrive in their own sizes and shapes,
brassy ones, classy ones, the agile and the slower,
this one lifts that one, on a shoulder one drapes,
another flies high, while this one is lower.
One soars as suspended from invisible rope,
some wear their glasses, others have braces,
all forming a kind of kaleidoscope
in which colours of all kinds merge and fill spaces.
So when you look out with those half-closed eyes,
the individuality it dies;
with focused look, more than a glance
you lose the dancers in the dance.

All budding womanhood is here, in all its various forms,
future mums and ministers combine with swots and flirts;
such infinite variety rules out any kind of norms
and means we see a foretaste of the joys and of the hurts
that wait for them and us in all that shared tomorrow;
but whatever we have left for them, we feel that these will cope

even in the midst of what brings pain and sorrow,
their joyful movement tells of something we call hope.
So when you look out on them with those half-open eyes
that individuality it dies;
with focused look, so much more than a glance,
you lose those dancers for the bigger dance.

THE WEDDING SCULPTURE

Time is carving out its sculpture today in here
that will be taken out and gazed on year on year.
All of us here present we shall keep it on the shelf
of our memories, and these two deep in the heart itself.
Long time from now, kept in the cupboard of the mind in dust,
it will be brought out by these two and they then must
see all it shows and tells them of this day in April ninety nine
so each can say, 'Then you gave me your love, and I gave mine.'
What will time's sculpture show, carved in and with such mutual love?
Captured for ever are their commitment, trust and yet above,
the oneness of a couple who are two but one,
a journey here just started, yet this day again begun.
We are lucky to have in our mind's archives, firmly dated,
such a unique piece of art that their true love created.

CAROLINE

(On the occasion of the twentieth anniversary of the raising of the
    Tibetan flag in Northampton)
On the Tibetan mountain tops where the clouds confuse us
and leave us wondering which world we're in,
the sturdy climbing boots we wear seem quite at odds
with the monks' sandals made of simple skin.
Perhaps their grip on what is really real
is surer than ours less certain as we must feel
with each cautious step we take and hesitate before our life's road
    bends,
as we watch out for blind alleys and dead ends.

At least our town can offer every kind of shoe and boot
to help us through the sorrow, joy and pain of every taken route.

I know of one from here whose looks suggest she knows
only of colour, style and lightness for her feet
to match the hair and eyes that strike you when you meet.
But in her heart she wears, as in her life she shows,
those sturdy boots that sometimes pinch and pain.
She knows those lofty clouds will not descend
so we must meet them to find some peace and gain
something of that inner serenity on which those loved depend.
She knows that weaving dreams is almost heavenly craft,
but that to make them here is down to earthly graft.
For twenty years the flag has risen with words aloud,
but words are breaths and may just float up to the cloud;
she shows in caring, trusting deeds that, yes, we can be led
to own each others' sorrows, and I can glimpse –through clouds-ahead,
I think that one day, when she will from us depart,
you may find 'LAMA' engraved upon her heart.

41

FOR JULIA —AFTER THREE MORE YEARS
OF BRANCH DIRECTOR SERVICE

'Can I help you?' It can sound so routine,
like someone at a counter or operating a machine.
But in this world of smartphones, laptops, all IT,
it's still the trueness in the voice that's key.
Perhaps it's who's behind the voice is what I mean
that makes some people different-just as it's always been.
They are the ones with extra heart that give
themselves to each one at a time; then they live
only at that moment for that other person's sorrow
shutting out their own –let that wait until tomorrow.

Among such few with that gift for such a task,
I know of one giving more than most of us could ask.
Like teachers, nurses and others in such fields,
the red tape of bureaucracy, it wields
a hammer above the heads of those who want to care,
saved only by those who take on more than their fair share.
They harness everyone's energy so that we don't lose sight
of the only thing that matters-that other person's plight.

So, thank you, Julia, yours really is a gift
to balance those two potential foes and in doing so to lift
the spirits of the listeners AND of those who call.
whatever praise we give you –you deserve it all.

THE HAT
(FOR AMBROSE)

I've never seen him anywhere without that same old hat;
it sits wide-brimmed across and round his craggy head,
on top a body that you can't think was ever fat.
For me, a kind of wisdom oozes out from every vein,
the kind that comes from motorcycling round the rocks of Crete,
being in trouble at home, then homeless on the street,
taking life's batterings full in the face-and giving some back again.
When, as for all of us, one day his life must reach its end,
I hope his last rites give that hat some pride of place,
because it'll carry the whole of him within its space.
Meantime, you don't need any help from me , my friend,
but I'll tell you now just what I'd like to do-
when I go and get a hat, I'll take it off to you!

THIS DAY
(ON A FRIEND'S WEDDING IN SOUTH AFRICA)

What is this day? This day is only
one of many gone and many yet to come.

And what of age, and race, country and such?
They can deter, but only in as much
that, faced with love, they are invisible and dumb.

For what is age but days, especially those ahead?
And what is country but where fate has had us bred?
And each of us has life with which to work, enjoy or cope.

What will this day look like from a future far?
Their love gives this day life and hope.

CHILDREN AND FAMILIES

THE PRIMARY SCHOOL – A CLASS
OF EARLY YEARS

'CHERRY TREE SCHOOL'- I read the name and I am gone
across the years to row on ragged row of unpruned, prolific trees.
My school of senses –and of life.
The smell of morning grass, the touch of the soft black globe
against the cheek, or rolling in the mouth before the juice's burst.
The shiny worn leather of the basket's belt,
the pause, then push of the first step up the day,
the roughness of the rung as you pull through the leaves,
and while I'm busy in the boughs,
the coarse chat of the country women- completes my tree of knowledge.

On entering the class, I see the picking season underway,
as workers hurry here and there carrying steps from tree to tree.
and all the baskets gradually are filled-
this one with coloured blocks, that one with paper leaves.
This one holds sand and water, constantly reformed,
that one a toilet rolled machine , elastic banded.
And watchful eyes and guiding hands check the crop,
guard the unripe ones and weigh the stock.
They know these pickers will look back,
not for the harvest –which is soon consumed-
but to the picking which is shaping them-as it did me.

AN UNBEARABLE RECEPTION

He sees the sign 'Reception', and steels himself for formal smiles,
painted nails and piled carpet, or liveries and lacquered hair,
musing whether it shall be sweet or dry, or maybe even medium,
carefully weighing the words to say when decisions are made,
he enters the room.

The world is uninhabited above his waist,
and as he hesitatingly absorbs the knee- high noise,
the Lilliputian hand that tugs his trouser leg, the finger tips,
seem to end in two frank eyes and one shrill voice,
'Look what I made!'

No escape now from admiring a garish but quite solid tower block,
tall, and even more so than its neighbours, so he's told.
Between and round his legs, they busily exclude him from their world;
here's one headphoned to another world; one cushioned in a dream.
He looks for teacher !

He takes in vivid colours-red, red, yellow, then more red,
surveying seaside, library, mini-Kew, and United Nations corner.
Tracing a Xylophonic 'ting', he focuses finally on the woollen rug.
Here's the teacher!

He politely asks her how she copes and so she tells,
but while she talks and he politely listens,
the fingertips and two frank eyes he sees again in his mind's eye;
he dares not ask her what he really wants to know,
'How can you bear all that trust?'

ON A PRIMARY SCHOOL CELEBRATING ITS TWENTY FIRST ANNIVERSARY

Listen. Close your eyes and listen
and you may hear
shouting and screaming, laughing and crying,
panting and gasping, scurrying and stamping,
all in that high pitched playground tone.
Listen carefully. You will hear
the pounding heartbeat of the first day child,
so loud that surely everyone can hear,
while first day mothers bustle back down the drive,
listening to their own heart's thumps and sniffles.

Listen while the volume falls
to a steady hum of pursed lipped application,
punctuated by a shout of 'My turn now!'
A whistle, clatter of cutlery and dishes, accompanying
    his guinea's worth of years.

The arithmetic's remorseless for them all.
Those of five are twenty six,
those of nine are thirty;
Dads who then were twenty nine now celebrate at fifty.
Mums who then were twenty six
now are forty seven;
Grandmas then of fifty nine have reached the stage of eighty.
Teachers too in middle twenties
some in their first post,
they are in their forties now=and still the children come!

Listen again and very carefully
and you may hear the future as the past.
As, many many years ahead,

a lone couple wandering
across a wintry landscape here
pause when the woman thinks she hears
a hum, a distant shout, a scream.
She wonders if it's her own heart beat
that sounds through the sharp air.
Or does it come with other distant noises,
from somewhere in the snow spread
thinly on the slopes they walk?

Her partner mentions how the place
was called 'White Hills' a long long time ago.
They listen but the noises fade away;
they hurry off to where their own children
await them at home-so noisily alive.

A CHILD'S VIEW OF THE STARS

They say that stars are other worlds than ours;
it may be so, but not to me.
They are part of our world, my world,
tiny speckles in the sharp plain dome
that safely covers me as I look up.

That hedge over there is my hedge,
that tree against the skyline is my tree,
the narrowing path stretching away from me is mine,
as is the ridge over which my lowest star flickers.

It seems that stretching out my hand-
I can touch my hedge, my tree, my ridge,
and on and upwards , I can touch my stars.

Do I feel they're mine something or someone
has placed this speckled dome over it all
to keep me and my world all safe?
Or are the stars telling me of things
beyond what my world needs to know?

I LOVE AUTUMN

I feel safe with Autumn.
It's as comforting as my old teddy bear
cast aside for a long time but always there for me to press against-
when no one's looking!

Dad's digging in Autumn!
Keen to push the first fork in and bend his back,
he takes down the old worn wellies from the garage rack,
first knocking them together to check for spiders-
when no one's looking!

The outside broom makes its appearance
to fight the everlosing battle of the leaves,
whipped and whisked from bough to kitchen door.
Potatoes now are had in sacks,
as if we're set for Winter's siege,
apples all yellowed and tinted
and put on shelves, and Mum's just hinted
she's making lists of woollen things-
when no one's looking!

Best of all, as now the leaves leave bare the hedge,
we find the birds' long departed nests.
No harm now to take them down
And see how they are made of Spring.
In one we find the seedless pulp
of hips and haws that gnawing field mice left at feed,
while chomping out its nutty seed.
Dad says to lift the nest up high
and if I can see through it to the sky,
then I can see next Spring-
and we are both looking!

SHE WANTS A RAINBOW-A TRUE STORY

Being Santa today at a Christmas Fayre,
raising money for the homeless; I'm doing my best.
Asking the next girl what she'd like as a gift,
'I'd like a rainbow-' I don't hear the rest.

How can I give her what she should have?
When I was her age, didn't I have my dreams?
She and her friends need those colours quite soon,
before it's too late-is it worse than it seems?
Can I replant the Amazon to what it was before?
Can I refreeze the ice caps to stop a flood?
Can I blow away the smog that's clogging the cities?
Or make sure the blue orchid will once again bud?

Can I help the Iberian lynx to re-breed ?
Or restore some coral to its former beauty?
Can I drive away the diesel, coal, all fossil fuel?
I am useless and helpless-I have failed in my duty.

Turning back to my queue in despair. 'Who's next here?'
'Now, what would you like for Christmas, my dear?'
'I'd like a doll---not a plastic one!' I'm told,
-and I just catch a glimpse of a small crock of gold.

ON THE NEW-BORN BABY

If in a few hours you can change
from slippery wrinkled bundle
to soft-skinned , wide-eyed being-
when I am an old wrinkled helpless bundle,
surely you will have changed the world;
already you have changed mine.

A FATHER'S HANDS

I've seen a hand that's twice the size of mine
firmly but gently pushing me aside
when I'm grabbing too soon to reach the struggling sheep;
I've seen those hands all dirt and blood
scrabbling the rocks to reach a bleat.

I've seen that hand rest firmly but with care
on the shoulder of my mother when she's low;
I've felt that hand smother both of mine.
Part of me wants to grow and become just like him,
the other wants to stay forever small- within my father's hands.

HIS MOTHER'S THIMBLE

She used to sit by the fire, darning box by her side,
either the knitting needles would be clicking,
rhythmically, speedily, endlessly,
or the darning needles would be flicking
in and out, relentlessly.

I remember the sights and the sounds,
I remember the tuts, the mutters or hiss
when a stitch was dropped or a finger pricked;
then out would come the thimble-yes, this-
to stay on her finger, helpfully.

I remember it all, with a pain like a knife,
for she was the woman in my life-
and I forgot to tell her I loved her.
Now she is long gone; the thimble is here,
the chair, and a few more momentoes,
just bits of that woman in my life,
the one I let down-now here is my wife.
So, I give you this thimble, my wife, and my love,
for, although you don't sew, please remember,
you are the woman in my life,
and I need to tell you both that I love you.

GRANDPARENTS

Once I broke my dad's best torch, exploring the universe under my bed.
I didn't tell Dad what I'd done, and went crying to Grandad instead.

Grandad said, 'Right, well, here's what we'll do,' and he bought one,
    down at the shop.
'No need to tell Dad', he quietly said-and Dad never noticed the swap.

Whenever I do something wicked, so bad that I can't tell my Mum,
Grandparents listen and go ,'Tut, tut!' but they always agree to stay
    dumb.
They're the best babysitters to have; eight o'clock is always nine-thirty!
And they don't poke around at your neck and your ears,
you can go off to bed-well, quite dirty!

And when I get older, and they are so old, too ancient to walk
    up the stairs,
if they want to tell me THEIR secrets, I promise I'll always
    keep theirs.

GRANDPARENTS ARE NOT ALWAYS OLD

Grandparents are not always old,
'She died aged fifty three.'
That's what it says on the gravestone,
shaded by hedge and tree.

I wasn't allowed at the funeral;
I was six when Grandma died.
I remember it as the only time
I saw my Dad had cried.

Now this fifty year old man grows cold,
but through the shadows he can see
just as I'm always six to her,
she will always be fifty three.

ALL SIZES OF EXPECTATIONS

The bride's father talks of episodes which moulded her for
　　this minute;
my son's groom's speech is funny and friends-focussed-I am
　　not in it.
I see my second son, also married just weeks ago, and I turn
to see these two fine grown men, waving or watching, and I yearn
to understand where I am now. Suddenly, I am not here,
I close my eyes a second and into the past I stare.

I am standing in a bedroom, its door is next to mine;
it has two beds, both small, the clock says something nine.
Two heads are on their pillows, both sets of hair are fair,
both faces lost, engulfed by sleep, at ease, their dreams elsewhere.
Never had I felt such love and, frighteningly, such power
for those two beings; my life, which in my own childhood's hour
had been so happy, though latterly, much emptiness,
now had its meaning in its purpose and hope of success,
some strong determination to ensure protection and a path ahead
which for the three of us could bring a thought each waking day
we'd anticipate that some good thing would likely come our way.
And in return-? No! Never 'in return', for nothing would they owe me.
My own return would come through their lives as they'd show me.
My life must find its own rewards, their feeling love for me perhaps;
for these two, I'd try not into hopes for myself to lapse.
I come back to the wedding's room, and smiling at the love
　　I finally found,
I realise the circle has come completely round.
Tonight, I'll see small vulnerable faces once again-
In one pushchair and two small beds, I'll feel both joy and pain
of expectations, hopes-and, looking at grandchildren's sleeping faces,
I'll know that none of us who care would ever be in any other's places.

SONNET FOR SAMANTHA
(A BELOVED STEPDAUGHTER)

I have come to be so glad our blood is not the same
so I can love you as a daughter, being free
from ties that sometimes bind us parents, such as blame
that maybe as a parent we should have loved them more,
and other duties that I found being a father brought.
Amidst the wildly happy times that words sometimes can't find,
came moments when ' I know I must' and, even more, 'I ought',
would make me try to feel what was the most appropriate.
If the words, 'I never asked to be born,' whether said or not,
sometimes hover there, with unspoken but unquestionable truth,
they can't intrude on anything that , from having you, I got.
Your beauty, talent- so much of your mother and my wife –
that we can talk together of 'the other woman' in my life!

TWO GRANDSONS
(SONNET FOR OLIVER AND ELLIOTT)

You have 'learning difficulties'-that's what they say,
but you are the best teachers we have ever had.
Something so wise came out of what at first seemed sad;
you taught us how to look at life a different way.
You made a decent loving woman and a man
into incredible parents surpassing any norm,
and grandparents who thought they knew the education form
into those who grasped a little more of this life's plan.
You are so special, yet you are still the same,
not as each other, for you each are your own you,
but like all of us, as we each seek our way through.
I think sometimes you best know the rules of this life's game!
As with all loves in our lives, there's something always yearning,
with this one, we can only hope to always go on learning.

TWO GRANDDAUGHTERS

Born three years and three thousand miles apart,
each of them has a special place within my heart.

Isabella, bright of smile and so very light of feet,
even her pout cannot disguise the fact she's sweet!
Her face so faunlike and so innocently eyed,
she can point and tap and sing and twirl and glide.
But she is more than what you see. Her restless mind
is searching for something, nearing womankind;
she stands at the door of what she does not know,
her fingers crossed, her hair uncertain of which way to blow.

Beatrice too has a winning smile, one that's hard to beat,
and all her spirit and her inner self find expression through
      her feet.
Her generous soul, evolved through family and teams,
means she can share with others as she claims her dreams.
Her restlessness of mind and body drives her ever to the ends
to ask the questions on which her future so depends.
Her outer loveliness comes from her deep inside
and shows in face and figure –without an ounce of pride.

But when they both move in their special spheres,
I see the baby's, girl's, and such young womanly years
all in one moving figure on the field and floor;
they are still there to me, and so much more.
Whilst moving, they are lost to me, and so should be,
they are themselves, have found themselves and I see
that in those movements they are both the same-
one IS the dance, the other IS the game.
Beatrice and Isabella, we do not ever own you;
ours is not to say you're ours, you're you.

We can only love you as you move away
and take on adult forms and functions day by day.
But I have something of you that you do not,
I have the 'you' of yesteryears you have not got.
Perhaps it all begins with son, daughter and mother?
Strange it is the more you pour all love into one other,
the more you have for others-it never falters,
such as that which I feel for these two granddaughters.

BO

Bo, you bring me such delight, with your shiny bright
eyes, your ear-to-ear smile, your turning to the light
which catches on your wayward hair. I see you there
upon the paths, upon the steps, upon the grassy slope where
leaves and grit make fascinating toys. I follow you there
and see you every few steps turn and show no fear.
Fear is what parents and grandparents have for you,
but you march on-with every hour, each day you grow.
I see the love in your father's eyes, in him too
I see a tiny toddler defenceless just like you.
I see your mother, anxious, so full of care,
we grandparents already to be ready to be there.
Bo, you are so loved, as yet you cannot know it-
all that the rest of us can do is show it.

THREE PICTURES OF LILLY

What have I seen?
I've seen a photo of a sweet-faced girl,
with a smile that looks beyond the camera's lens,
into a world she knows is hers, and it's her friend.
She holds a doll in one arm and over in the other
a floppy rabbit, of which she's also mother.
This is a child ready for bed and dreams
In which she finds her innocence is everything it seems.

What do I see?
I see another photo of a girl who is still sweet,
but thoughtful now, almost as if she's learned to feel;
the rabbit she holds no longer floppy but is real.
She's been a mermaid and she's flown a kite;
into her lengthening life has come a light.
She's seen the wild woods, and the tiger's been to tea;
'What next?' she seems to say. 'What has life got for me?'

What will I see?
I think I'll see a photo of a young woman who
has not only lived and loved but has learned too.
She's learned that while she's pretty and looks sweet,
the tigers in the real world might turn on her to eat!
But I think I'll see her nature with the courage to be strong;
I think she'll find her place somewhere, a place where she'll belong.

THE GIRL AND THE MERMAID

In a man's rowing boat, out on the water,
watching the ripples from the oars cascade,
sat the pretty girl, the man's granddaughter,
and these thoughts around her mind they played.

'I wish I could be a mermaid so,
with my own top half but a silver tail,
I'd swim right down to the depths below
and watch the boats above me sail'.

Then a sudden splash, leaving barely a trace,
made the girl peer right down into the water.
She could just make out a shape and a face
that amazed that girl, the pretty granddaughter.

For what she saw was her very own face,
but with a silver tail that made a swish.
She knew at once –in that very place-
that it had come true-her special wish.

She looked again, but no mermaid was there;
gone back to the rocks where the fishes float,
where she would sit and comb her hair,
dreaming perhaps of the girl in the boat.

The girl looked up; a voice could be heard;
'Margot, it's time for go home,' it said.
Her secret that people would say was absurd,
she'd hug it close to her each night in bed.

VULNERABILITY AND CARE

SYMPHONY FOR THE THIRD AGE

There IS a beauty in this place of life's third age.
I see them sitting-always sitting- in a kind of row,
like a chorus line resting after a lifetime's show,
and in their faces you can see the present and the past,
those that they were and that which will always last.
What you see now for some is sad serenity in places,
but stirred by timeless twinklings and flittering smiles on faces.

These women still hold the secret of true love;
it sits beside them and behind them in their row,
those they have loved, love still, and who love them now.
A clasped hand which fears to let her slip away,
a studied look of 'I'll be here if you sleep all day'.
These need no words which once their youth asked for.
In uniform or not, the room is full of love –and more.

And the future? This is tomorrow and next week,
for this kind of beauty does not ask for more.
Many tomorrows and next weeks are for some in store.
I came expecting to be sad in seeing pain;
I leave assured, knowing that when I come again,
I'll see what life here makes impossible to miss-
there IS a beauty in a place like this.

STANDING IN THE GARDENS AT SYMPHONY HOUSE

As I stand in the gardens of the nursing home here,
which, at front , back and side, they almost surround,
I take in the brightness and the colours of the flowers;
it seems as I have been musing here for hours-
I'm able to see the beauty in the round,
In what in fact is minutes since I came to peer.

In fact, like much of beauty, it is hard won.
Each plant is tended, nourished, given adequate room,
what harms is removed, to take away any fear;
the work goes on caselessly, all though the year.
New plants are admitted, roots put down, mostly bloom,
an occasional loss means a space for this new one.

As I force myself to move away from selfish pleasure,
thinking of those inside who'll greet me with smiles,
I'm conscious that as I turn back to the building,
the work that goes on there is tough and unyielding;
the tenderness and brightness there, it so beguiles
that I forget that I'm lucky that I stand here at leisure.

The lightness and brightness, both outside and in
are achieved both through love and the effort put in.
Does it matter which mirrors which, I wonder?
No –both people and flowers cast this spell that I'm under.

A MOMENT IN THE NURSING HOME

'I'm not much of a one for talking,' said the grey-haired woman in the
     chair,
'but I used to sing in the choir, you know,
a while ago now. I've forgotten how.'
'Did you, dear? That's nice,' said a nurse as she tried to prepare
the table for tea.
'Now, let me see.
I think it might like this go.'

The two nurses smiled at each other, and the manager he smiled too,
as the woman went to clear her throat.
Then out came a sound that's only ever been found
in the finest of concerts, cathedrals, and echoing through
their roofs and rafter
with joy trailing after,
like the purest of notes as they float.

The mouths in the room had dropped open; there was silence
     everywhere.
As this woman of eighty seven
with a voice as if from heaven
it had come to earth to give birth
to such beauty in which could share.

That moment of bliss from such source, I wish I could hold it for ever,
but can I ever forget it? The answer is certainly – never!

THE VISITOR TO THE NURSING HOME

She came to the home; her youth had gone by.
She felt that her beauty had fled.
But I could see through a look in her eye
that sparkled like stars in the sky
her spirit was a long way from dead.

She was a strange person, with whom none could compare,
there was something you could not quite tell;
each day she grew younger while she was there,
her hair which was grey became fair-
like others, I fell under her spell.

After nine or ten months, being younger each day,
she got out of her chair and she said,
'You've given me your time, now I must away;
the years are against me, I cannot delay;
someone else can have my room and bed'.

Next morning, quite empty her room and her chair;
no one could remember her name.
they searched high and low; no one was there,
not a hair of her head, grey or fair.
Things seemed to go on just the same.

Was she from heaven, or perhaps outer space,
this woman who refused to grow old?
Was she real, or a ghost, or a heavenly grace,
who came among us here in this place?
Was she from where it's hot or it's cold?

Some other women had been moved to complain
how much older they felt in that year.
Has she gone elsewhere some more time to regain?
Will she steal back to cause yet more pain?
No one says, but it's what they all fear.

She vanished as if she had never been there;
surely more than a trick of the light.
Some say that she floats in the cold morning air;
that she laughs out loud, others swear.
Perhaps she comes back in the night?

THE MAN AT THE RAILWAY STATION

He stood right at the edge of the platform, as if in some kind of trance.
His eyes were glued to the tracks below,
as if somehow he didn't quite know
what was the next step to take in life's dance.

The voice came over the speaker, 'Please keep well back from the line.
The next train doesn't stop here.'
But he showed no fear
as he stood like a statue, the hand trembling was mine.

I reached out and touched his elbow-he rounded on me with a start.
He gave me such a look,
the force of it shook
my whole being as both our worlds fell apart.

That look seemed to say to my conscience I'd robbed him of what he'd
been sure.
Those tracks were so straight,
he was sure of his fate,
because of my well-meaning gesture, he'd have to face many days more.

I saw him no more at the station, but I've seen others like him
elsewhere,
I'm still really unclear
If they're better off here,
or if they know where they're going, should I let them go there?

THE NIGHT CALLER

'I don't want this life, but I don't want to die.
I know you'll hear this from others tonight.
I'm numb inside and I wish I could cry,
please stay with me till at least it's light.

I want this pain to end, the abuse, all this sorrow;
but do I want to leave it all for ever?
Do I really want there to be no tomorrow?
It's nothing to do with being stupid or clever;
it's the emptiness, the vacuum, the nothing to hope;
each day I go into this same cul-de-sac
where the only way out are those pills or this rope,
yet I must go forward, for there's no going back.

I'm told there are options, but I see no choice,
I just see more of the same-I have even prayed-
all I can hear is this inner voice
saying, 'Go on, do it! Don't be afraid!'

But I AM afraid- of two things-first the pain,
then the knowledge that I will not wake up again.
The whole thing I see in this contradictory light-
suicidal thoughts helped me through this night.

I'LL WIN TOMORROW

Tomorrow, I know, will be my lucky day.
I just know for certain-whatever they say.
After so many losses, I'm due a big win
and I'm certain tomorrow my luck will be in.

I remember my last win-yes, I see them frown;
I put it all on the next chance, but that went right down.
But that was just bad luck, so I laid out some more.
Now I've got creditors banging my door.

Yes, I also know that I once had a wife
and many other things so precious in life.
But they didn't understand each time that I lost;
and now, on my own, I am counting the cost.

They begged me to stop and I briefly did,
but really I don't need to be seen as a kid.
Though I've almost no money, I can stop when I please-
it'll take only one win for my troubles to cease.

So, don't think I can't stop, because I'm sure I can;
I'm stopping tomorrow-to show I'm a man.
That's after one more go, one more bet to play-
tomorrow, you see, will be my lucky day.

A NEARLY KIND THING

I woke up in the doorway and I felt pretty bad,
then, all of a sudden , there in front was this lad.
'Are you okay?' he mumblingly said.
'I've got no money, but I wish that I had.'
'That's alright, son,' I said. 'I'll be okay.
What 's your name, son?' But before he replied,
three other boys ran up and shoved him aside.
'Come on, you dope-don't worry about him;
he's dirty and smelly and probably dim!'
The boy went all red and off they all shot.
He glanced over his shoulder and what I got
was a feeling that he was embarrassed because
he'd been caught being kind and my feeling was
I felt sorry for him, though I'm in a bad way,
and I'd rather be me than those others, though they
might be alright on their own, I suppose,
but when you need kindness-well, that's how it goes!
But just for a second, well, he cared about me,
I'll remember him always, you just wait and see.

LOOKING FOR HOPE

When you're cooking a meal, say, for someone you love,
you put into the process those very same feelings;
choose the best fruit and veg, serve it up from above,
why give any thought to those thrown away peelings?

That's what I feel like, not that best, but that waste
that even the Council doesn't want on its patch.
The bully gangs mock me-they love the power they taste.
Everyone is against me-no, wait-there's the catch!
When you're at rock bottom, nowhere lower to go,
you start blaming others, lashing out at them all,
but, after, you look at yourself and think, 'No-
I'm playing the lead in MY story, though small.'

What is the point?' and 'Why bother being here?'
What stops me from ending and what gives me scope
for just keeping going, specially this time of year,
to be honest, I'll tell you –a big small thing called hope!

Hope's when a woman actually asks for my name,
and when he shakes my hand as if I were real.
Hope is when anyone shows I'm the same
by discussing an issue- 'Well, what do you feel?'
Wary smiles from those passing as they take the wide view.
Hope's in the copper's, 'How you doing this morning?'
Hope's in the vicar who lets me sleep in a pew.
Hope tastes like this coffee someone brought me at dawning.

In my darkest days, these small glimmers of light
help me to see there could be a point in tomorrow,
a reason to rise, drag me out of this plight,
stop me sinking back into my self-sounding sorrow.
Someone told me of somewhere of which someone had heard-
I found it-that place-it's called and gives –Hope!

REFLECTIONS

ON LOOKING AT A PAINTING
OF AN AUTUMN SCENE

The stream emerges from the black- back there.
It widens as it flows towards the watcher- me!
Reversing nature's seasonal pattern, the golden splurged brown
of the still fully clothed trees reassures us Libran folk.
We see this Autumn not as a prelude to what's darkly spaced,
but more the culmination of a journey that we've faced.
one that's had its steps back, slips and trips, and even at times
a by-road, where a treacherous dead end made us shrink.
Those steps I see remind me that we've had to climb
before we gain what we Autumnals like to think
of as kind of peace; not one of indolence or wasting time,
but one of coming to terms with what's been put in our way,
one that tells of greenness past, even of an over brightly day.
But these mottled hues of russet gold and brown I see,
they are not faded brightness but just in a quieter sun,
as you and I are in our Autumnal phase of two as one.
Perhaps I'd claim wherein the real gold in that brownness lies?
Is it- I hope- a little bit of growing not old but wise?

GARDEN POPPIES

The poppies in my garden do not seem like those of Flanders Field;
There are not many of them and they're far too heavy at the top,
As if they'd gorged on their own glory till they had to stop.
I'm almost disappointed in them for their rather melancholy yield.
Until at last and suddenly, they spill their contents out, not on the
     ground,
but surprisingly in softly scarlet petals, revealing that once hidden black,
so long kept secret, as if pleasure's gained from having been held back.
Yet, all too soon, each petal falls away, leaving that black open all
     around.
I pick up feathery petals, leaving the deepest black at heart that I expose.
I wish that I could put those petals back, and cover up that inner sore;
I wish I'd asked my long gone grandfather so much more.
Just for a moment, I understand why poppies matter to the families of
     those
who only had the blackness left, though a little softened by years passed.
It's much too late for questions of such a personal dimension,
but not of course for others, like ones about conflict that we rarely
     mention,
why are there some who seem to want to make the blackness last?
Too late for all those Grandads-no message to them can I write or send,
only my watering eyes can make a feeble, quite inadequate amend.

A SINGLE PRIMROSE

There's a single primrose growing in my patch of unmown grass,
and I'm secretly quite proud of this bit of my little scheme
to grow a mini-meadow here so I can make it seem
like a miniature of childhood days, if it ever comes to pass.

We picked primroses from woods and fields by the score
and carried them home in bunches, tied up with darning wool,
thinking of the vases-and jamjars-that soon would be so full,
especially on that Sunday, so Mum would know for sure
that we did know she cared for us, because we didn't have the words.
Violets too we carried in smaller bunches of blue,
cowslips and oxlips were left alone-somehow we always knew
that some things were forbidden, like eggs from smaller birds.

Were we to blame that nowadays many fewer wild flowers grow?
And, if we were, why then-how could anybody know?
Were we to blame as those who ploughed up the meadows' grass?
As those who fenced in the open woods of nut trees and the beeches,
beneath which the bluebells grew-never picked, as nature teaches,
as those who mowed the verges for the motorist to speed past?

I'm keeping my primrose company in my messy meadow scene,
And I hope next year perhaps there might be two or three.
A tiny step for me, for my children maybe more.
But my children's children, I can't know, what will they have seen?

WHAT THE ROBIN TAUGHT ME

I learned the future from my workmate robin,
though it took some time for my slow human mind
to realise what he'd shown me over a long time,
that the tiny cultivated piece of earth was more his than mine.
So often had he and I worked together,
in most seasons, whatever the weather,
that I'd grown to think of us as a kind of team
that was manging it, keeping everything in line.

When it dully dawned on me that, though each year he seemed the
    same,
he was in fact an outcome of last year's courting game,
thus he and I were just the latest in our respective lines,
I knew that my half of our stewardship would end one day.
But it gave me some comfort that our work together made some sense,
for he could teach potential heirs in his own special way.
Though I might have eighty, ninety years and he but one,
my time there was much shorter; he had generations still to run.

A BUSY DAY !

I sat in the garden drowsily, on a hot July day,
too lethargic to move from my chair.
Tasks to be done were in my head, far away:
'ought to do' kept me rooted there.

Two butterflies fluttered near, just for me to see.
'Only cabbage whites,' I say, while they landed and tasted
the multi-flowered bloom of the buddleia tree-
so this day is not being wasted.

A furry bee whirring and busy now hovers within my sight,
descends to the snapdragon's welcome again,
then flies off somewhere else to alight-
so this day will have not been in vain.

A spider, boldly spotting my convenient self,
and to lose any work's chance being loth,
starts its web from my static shoulder in stealth
-so this day is not solely for sloth.

I'm sure that under that stone near my rest,
a thousand ants are busy working away,
burrowing, breeding, building another industrious nest
-so all's not being wasted today.

I doubt any of my puny efforts today
could match these creatures' work's worth;
perhaps we'd be wise to keep out of their way
-and let them do what is best for their earth.

MASTER AND SERVANT

There's no 'Excuse me' in a cat.
Except to be of use to him,
I have no other life but that.

Deludedly, I sit on a garden seat
In lordly fashion stretching out my legs,
wth my master at my feet.

I'm allowed to bend and stroke his fur,
languorously extended on his back-
then a flutter of white and instant stir-
a flash and a dash of every nerve and sinew;
butterfly missed, lazy return, roll over-
and a look which says-'You may continue!'

RAIN PLAYS ITS PART

Stamping in the puddles in the country lanes, aged four,
waiting at the stop for a girl to get off the bus in March,
gazing at grass too wet for cutting on a dreary day
in a life when that might offer some relief from lovelessness;
walking in its driving force on Sundays waiting for things to change,
sitting in a car , eating homemade sandwiches which taste so much
of new found faith in a future which will see these showers out.

Sifting through memories and not trying to make sense,
the rain insists upon its place in these pictures of the past,
yet not, it seems, in any but a positive way.
Even a youthful football match played on sodden pitches
cannot compare with the excitement of the wetness beating
on my face and on hers too at times. There is a thrill in this
potential in the rain-the force that floods and savages some homes,
yet strokes the grass in early mornings to produce that scent.
Just watch that single drop move so slowly down the window pane;
surely it doesn't know I cannot wait for it to rain again!

FEBRUARY 2020

Is it winter still, or can this new day be Spring?
The trees seem undecided:
some still stand in all their splendid starkness,
against the contradictorily blue sky with white,
while others almost skittishly offer their leaves
for the bright afternoon sun to bounce and play upon.
Yet the wintry wind will not let go without a fight.
It forces its chilly way inside your coat
and flattens the challenging shrub against the garden wall.
It rattles the garage door like some unholy wraith,
daring those defiers in their thinking that the sun is here to stay.

A blackbird flits along the grass,
sensibly seeking the shelter of that Victorian wall,
with its long experience of wind and sun and rain and more.
But I'll trust the robin, my workmate and familiar,
that when I venture out to cut back a bit of wintry growth,
and show whose side I'm on to welcome warmth,
that, if he joins me, I'll know it's safe to plant new hope.

THE WHOLE THING

Like in a Lowry, scurrying figures make no sense,
until you see the picture as a whole.
Constable's individual trees are flawed,
but his world of green is full of soul.
So, in my garden, putting in carefully chosen flowers
gives me the colour for a selfish pleasure,
but only when I step back and see my scene,
when I've forgotten planting and am at leisure
then I can see there's something here outside of me,
and though I've put in cuttings here and there,
it's the 'me' that's in that whole that I can see.
Criticism picks apart, missing the essence of the art;
the whole we see and feel, but with the heart.

FINE!

Even good husbands at times
can commit the most terrible crimes.
A particular bugbear of mine
is when they say something is 'fine'.

Now you cook them a delicious dinner,
each course you just know is a winner;
after pudding, you pour out the wine,
you say, 'How was that?' They say, 'Fine!'

You're going out to a very posh dance,
you spend hours at the mirrors, askance,
from hairdo to tiptoe, you are dressed to the nine;
you say 'How do I look?' They say, 'Fine!'

You buy them a great birthday present,
wrap it up to look even more pleasant;
you know it's the thing for which they pine;
you say, 'Do you like it?' 'It's fine!'

The next time he does it, I swear,
I'll murder him, no matter where.
I'll tell them I came to the end of the line-
when they take me away, I'll say 'Fine!'

I LOVE YOU, BOOK

Book, my book. Why do I love you, book?
Of course you tell me lots, I learn from you,
I'm a different person when I'm done with you.
But I can get all this in other forms-
Like voice and even shiny screens;
perhaps, just maybe, it's something in your look.

Ah, yes, your look. Nothing else has quite your look.
But also, when we're close, your smell, the feel, the touch,
like paper, vellum, card, gilt edge, or cellophane,
and even as you age, become spotted, browned crinkled,
wrinkled, edges faded, sagging, and turned down,
I love you just as much and more, you book.

When I hold you in my hands, you book,
I run them over you and pass from hand to hand,
and even take your outer cover off to see your pristine self beneath.
But while I fondle you, I need to know about you when we're done.
You'll soon be on the shelf with all my other loves,
so that I, the lover, can give you all that look!

But before that happens, we'll go to bed, my book,
and snuggle down together for the night.
And when I tire, I'll gently put you to one side,
turn out the light and know that you'll be there for me
when I wake, ready for me whenever I have need.
It sounds just like eternal love might look!

But no, I'm not content, I'm too promiscuous, my book.
When I have done with you and put you on that shelf,
I'll find another and take it in my care and hands;
so it also becomes another love, and ends up just the one.

I love you all, so many, and some so many times
that I can scarce remember which one I lastly took.

And if YOU too, like me, love books,
then you and I are lovers, you are shameless too,
in loving, leaving, loving yet again.
Yes, you and me and all of us are lovers through and through.

BODIES

'And over here,' said the guide, as she showed us around,
'are some jawbone shavings that were recently found
in the wastebins of clinics, with spare fat and the rest
of excesses of some people's bottoms and breast'.
As the droning goes on in the tour of this place,
I reflect on my body, its limbs and my face.
It's not even been sculpted or filtered or trimmed
and-whisper it now-it's not even been slimmed!
Am I one of the last generation to feel
that the body I was born in is the one that is real?
But 'real' is not good, it's old-fashioned and twee-
it's like using the coins of an old currency.

The guide is now telling us of the progress we've made.
'We've got rid of the menopause , and no one is afraid
of ageing or being out of synch with their peers'.
All around me is glamour, so where are my fears?
If toxic babes menstruate before they are seven,
and US girls begin puberty before they're eleven,
and then we don't age, we look better and fitter,
there's only one outcome for our human litter.
Dying won't be an end, just a nuisance, a drag.
Let's rent a womb, buy a part in a bag.
Forget any worries we'll be like father or mother;
after all, we won't really tell one from another.
Ah well, I shall die, and when I'm in my grave,
They can put up a headstone on which they'll engrave,
'Here lies a man who was all flesh and bone,
but at least he had feelings and a mind of his own'.

THE WASP ON THE STAIRS

Today, I found a wasp, half comatose upon the stair
-a wasp- in the middle of November!
Surely it should have died in those Summer months
-perhaps so long ago, it can't remember.
And now it tries half heartedly to move ,
hardly knowing whether it has life or wing.
Yet still I hesitate to pick it up at all,
Wondering if there's still something in its sting.

And is that me, something not knowing where it is?
A creature out of tune and out of time?
Are these verses doomed to lie and die,
hemmed in by structure and by rhyme?
Perhaps –and yet, just like the wasp, I'll fight
to try to tell whoever cares to hear
that some things live and change and die,
while others show us that it's always here.
I need to tell myself, over and again,
of the one thing constant in us all.
In all the speed and hassle of today,
if we just pause, we'll hear it softly call-
that still voice that poets and painters understand
when it tells them what they have to do,
to show the world as how the voice is showing them
and forget what fashions and fame pursue.
Just like this wasp perhaps, half comatose upon the stair,
sometimes, I am unsure which way us up or down.
The wasp it will not last –perhaps few minutes more.
I do not know how long I'll wait in limbo there,
but I'll go on reaching out to others,
before I reach the top- or bottom - stair.

NO GOING BACK

Odd how the memories of my childhood years
seem all to come to me in black and white.
Some would say
they should be grey
because of rationing of colour in those post-war fears.
My mother always reaching for her old box brownie,
loved by her, as we were, closely held it seemed for ever.
Well, looking at it all, in starkest white and black,
and, seeing my life now, I would not go back.

Then, early years of a first own home and sons
and first footings on a path of responsible career
brought such knowing
with children growing
in my father's fierce love for first 'other' ones.
The understanding of that otherness in life,
helping to see what's missing, as well as what was had.
Well, looking at that time, seeing what I had to lack,
And seeing my life now, I would not go back.

Then middle years brought me, while not seeking,
An even fiercer love, one made me complete.
Rose-tinted views
on which I muse?
No, because that intensity of love was beyond peaking;
that love and passion stays inside me and it will
be remoulded, reshaped, but never lose its inner self.
And yet, looking at my life as it is now, nothing to lack,
no, even to that time I would not go back.

Well, maybe, it's as well, because I can't!
I've had so many things, all new and still

97

New ones emerge
as ideas surge,
into my mind from earlier seeds that plant
themselves , need to be watered and brought on.

And yet-and yet- although I would not go back
to a world of any colour, even one of white and black,
all my life's experiences cannot help me-they just mock,
because they have not taught me how to stop life's clock.

NOT BECAUSE OF ME

When I was born, a big war broke out;
but I can't think it was because of me.
There were too many tyrants with power to wield,
jostling for position, and dividing up nations
to have any time for one baby boy born
in a remote village, near orchard and field.

When about five, there were great celebrations,
but I can't think they were meant for me.
There were too many winners all out for some gain,
sharing out countries and displacing peoples
to think about one boy who was just starting school,
finding a strange father who'd come home again.
When I was near thirty, men landed on the moon,
but I can't think they went there for me.
When I saw the flags planted on that planet's floor,
I knew the tyrants were too busy plotting
to have any time for a man making his way
along usual pathways that lay behind and before.

When I neared to fifty, a great wall came down,
But I can't think they broke the barrier for me.
In all the cheering and shouting 'We're free!'
the tyrants were plotting to carve out new nations
to have any time for one middle-aged man
who'd learned life's routines and new futures could see.

Now, I'm near to eighty and the world's in a rage,
but I can't think it can ever matter to me.
More tyrants in power, in places quite new,
but I know now that to love and be me within
is the way we'll survive, whilst remembering that
we are many in number and the tyrants are few.

ON DOUBLE TIME

I tell you, they won't get this player off the stage!
Sometimes in loving lust, I'm forty four again,
or, lasting longer, when the sunlight bounces off the holly leaves,
or when the garden's grass smells wetly from the dawning rain,
then I'm as sure as anyone can ever really be
my life here it can never end, and each tomorrow is the same,
when I'm greedily grasping this small world of mine,
leaving nil for others, beyond perhaps a modicum of fame.

Each day shows us double-crossing, double-counting time.
You may try to count it by the calendar or clock,
but the time that counts is the one you feel as real,
like when the one you love is away , when it will mock
you with making your ten minutes seem an hour,
or, lost in pleasure, your hours are gone in seconds-
but I know deep down, over time clock-bound I have no power.

COMING HOME

I've lived in eleven houses, and I've had two homes.
First was our 'cottage', a tumbledown kind of place,
with no running hot water, a tin bath and a copper,
with one open fire and two rooms upstairs.
A ceiling so low
That as I grow
I have to stop down to enter the room,
With a paraffin lamp, then a candle for bed.
What a great day it was when the 'lectric man came,
put in two sockets
and a switch for a light.
No phones of course but a call box in the village,
a mile to the shop, and a bus twice a day.
This was a home-it could never reject,
there was a sense of healthy loving neglect.
When not outside, with friends in the lanes,
I would stare at the fire, see all life in its flames.
With my candle, I'd read stories into the night,
till Mum must have come in and turned out the light.

I can see now that I have come home;
as I gaze at the flames-they're not real ones today-
they stir up their life and with it stir mine.
Same feeling of place newly wrapped around me,
with the woman I love whom I finally found.
We can give to each other, after passion and fervour,
the whole of ourselves, nothing to reject,
but still with that loving healthy neglect,
leaving me to be me and she to be she.
As a child, it's all there
just because it is there,
now as a grandparent I am so aware
of the time that is left as well as what's gone.
So I ponder the questions a child needn't ask.

I've bought and I've lived in 'three beds', even 'four',
I often felt I'd arrived but never really got there.
I've found for myself that there's only one test-
when a home closes round you, you forget all the rest.
Sometimes, I come home and I'll switch on the light,
and when a bulb blows, I'll probably curse.
While I search for a new one, I'll just recall
the paraffin lamp, and there on the shelf
see the old candle holder
now sixty years older;
and I know if I lit up its wick, I would see
the candle just winking
with both of us thinking
of those shared secrets that ended in dreams.
In my years left, I've little yearning to roam-
the candle holder has told me that I have come home.

MY FAREWELL

Those of you who love me, try not too much to grieve,
you and I will have taken perhaps just a short leave.
Tomorrow, when you wake, I am still in your heart,
and, for the rest of your life's short stay, it is the start
of my new life with you, but in a different form.

I am in the clearness of the air after a storm,
the scent of new cut grass after a summer shower,
in the skies that hold your eyes at the dusking hour,
the tender roughness of the fruit trees' boughs and bark.
They are all me for you, sometimes in light , or yet in dark.

But also in the shuffling of the pages of a book,
and in my children and their children, you will see a look;
you'll hear a laugh, a groan, a quotation and a jest,
all these and many more. You all do have the rest
of your lives with me. My love for you's still here;
though my body's gone, I'm with you year on year.

Lightning Source UK Ltd.
Milton Keynes UK
UKHW041910080620
364668UK00001B/85